THE WORLD CUP 1991
RUGBY SONGS
&
DITTIES

Joint Editors
Scott Milway & Jamie Macleod-Johnstone

ISBN 1 873491 05 0
First published in 1991
Copyright Expandgood Ltd.
2, The Square, Richmond, Surrey, TW3 3DY

Printed in Great Britain by
Vine & Gorfin Limited, Exmouth, Devon

ACKNOWLEDGEMENTS

This book would never have been compiled without Eric Williams and his ex-patriate friends who produced the original 'Lagos Rugby Club Ditties' whilst working in Nigeria in 1958. We would like to thank him for his consent, allowing us to bring an updated second edition into the 1990s. The joint editors would also like to thank Smokey Cole for his entertaining cartoons, much appreciated additional material from Ken Aplin and Dai Gabriel, and to Janie Macleod-Johnstone, Sheila Burns and Joy David, whose blushes have not been spared and their vocabulary increased, whilst putting this second edition together.

This book was designed to produce laughter and more importantly to present Children in Need with a large cheque. We would like to thank, therefore, the innumerable pubs, clubs, factories, shops and people who have helped us sell the book.

All information is included by the editors in good faith and is believed to be correct at the time of going to press. No responsibility can be accepted for error.

INTRODUCTION

God made Little Boys
He made them all of String
He had a little over so
He made a Little Thing.
God made Little Girls of
Ribbon and of Lace,
He hadn't quite enough so
He left a Little Space.
Thank God

The rhyme gently points out the two sources which, since the beginning of mankind, have provided a never-ending stimulus for the imagination of men, especially rugby men, to create the songs and ditties combined in this collection and for the pleasures to which they sometimes allude. They have been handed down from generation to generation with embellishments at every turn.

We make no excuses for compiling what is probably the rudest book in the market place! It is quite unashamedly unabridged. Every song and ditty included has been selected for its intellectual obscenity. It is typically British, part of our folklore and an excuse to let rip on the ribald humour men love whether it is sung in the bar after a game, around the barbecue at a party, around the piano in a pub or in remote English speaking communities around the world.

In cold print the songs are almost impotent but bellowed out by a group of powerful men they come into their own and will continue to live on, being updated by each generation, as long as men gather together after a game.

We hope you enjoy this collection; we look forward to the next edition with additions of new versions from players, clubs and spectators around the globe, whose contributions will be gratefully acknowledged.

USE AND ABUSE OF THIS BOOK

THE LIMERICKS

You will find the many limericks in this book at the sign of the Leprechaun as shown here. These can be sung in the traditional 'Sing us another one do' style.

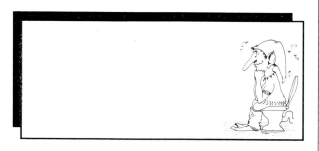

THE SONGS

We have deliberately, in the main, omitted suggesting tunes for the songs in this collection. Some are traditional, others will be sung to the reader's own interpretation: we have no wish to confuse people!

THE CARTOONS

Smokey Cole's cartoons follow the theme of the match before, during and after the game. Please see the special order form at the back of the book which enables you to purchase these cartoons in colour. They are available individually or as a collection with names of players, colleagues or anyone you think they may resemble.

INDEX

FIVE MINUTES TO GO

Whoredean School

We are from Whoredean,
Whoredean girls are we,
We take no pride in our virginity,
We take precautions
And avoid abortions
For we are from Whoredean School.

CHORUS

Up school, up school, f**k the school,
La, la, la, la, la, la, la, la, la, hoi.
La, la, la, two fingers up your crutch.

Our house mistress you cannot beat,
She lets us go walking in the street.
We sell our titties for threepenny bitties
Right outside Whoredean School.

CHORUS

Our school doctor, she is a beaut,
Teaches us to swerve
When our boy friends shoot.
It saves many marriages
And forced miscarriages,
For we are from Whoredean School.

CHORUS

Our head prefect, her name is Jane,
She only likes it now and again,
And again and again,
And again and again,
And again and again and again.

CHORUS

We go to Whoredean, don't we have pluck,
We go to bed without asking a buck.
Try us sometime boys,
You may be in luck.
For we are from Whoredean school.

CHORUS

Our sports mistress she is the best,
Teaches us to develop our chest.
So we wear tight sweaters,
And carry French letters.
For we are from Whoredean school.

CHORUS

We are at Whoredean each Whitsun dance.
We don't wear bras
And we don't wear pants.
We like to give our boy friends a chance,
For we are from Whoredean school.

CHORUS

Our school porter he is a fool.
He's only got a teeny weeny tool.
Its all right for key holes
And for little girl's peeholes,
But no good for Whoredean School.

CHORUS

Our school gardener he makes us drool.
He's got a great big, whopping, dirty tool.
All right for tunnels
And Queen Mary funnels,
And for the girls of Whoredean school.

CHORUS

We go to Whoredean, don't we have fun.
We know exactly how its done.
When we lie down we hole it in one,
For we are from Whoredean school.

CHORUS

We have a new girl, her name is Flo,
Nobody thought that she could have a go,
But she surprised the vicar
By raising him quicker
Than any other girl at Whoredean school.

CHORUS

These girls from Cheltenham,
They are just sissies.
They get worked up over one or two kisses.
It takes wax candles,
And long broom handles,
To rouse the bowels
Of girls from Whoredean school,

CHORUS

We go to Whoredean, we can be had.
Don't take our word, boy,
Ask your old dad.
He brings his friends
For breath-taking trends;
For we are from Whoredean school.

CHORUS

When we go down to the sea for a swim,
The people remark on the size of our quim.
You can bet your bottom dollar,
It's as big as a horse's collar,
For we are from Whoredean school.

Dinah

A rich girl has a limousine;
A poor girl has a truck.
But the only time that Dinah rides,
Is when she has a f**k.

CHORUS

Dinah, Dinah, show us your leg,
Show us your leg,
Show us your leg,
Dinah, Dinah, show us your leg,
A yard above your knee.

A rich girl has a brassiere,
A poor girl uses string.
But Dinah uses nothing at all
She lets the bastards swing,

CHORUS

A rich girl has a ring of gold,
A poor girl one of brass.
But the only ring that Dinah has
Is the one around her arse.

CHORUS

A rich girl uses vaseline,
A poor girl uses lard.
But Dinah uses axle-grease
Because her c**t's so bloody hard.

CHORUS

A rich girl uses a sanitary towel,
A poor girl uses a sheet.
But Dinah use's nothing at all,
Leaves a trail along the street.

If I were the Marrying Kind

If I were the marrying kind,
Which I thank the Lord I'm not, Sir,
The kind of man that I would wed
Would be a rugby full-back.

And he'd find touch and I'd find touch,
We'd both touch together,
We'd be all right in the middle of the night
Finding touch together.

If I were the marrying kind,
Which I thank the Lord I'm not, Sir,
The kind of man that I would wed
Would be a wing three-quarter.

And he'd go hard and I'd go hard,
We'd both go hard together,
We'd be all right in the middle of the night
Going hard together.

If I were the marrying kind,
Which I thank the Lord I'm not, Sir,
The kind of man that I would wed
Would be a centre three-quarter.

And he'd pass it out and I'd pass it out,
We'd both pass it out together,
We'd be all right in the middle of the night
Passing it out together.

If I were the marrying kind,
Which I thank the Lord I'm not, Sir,
The kind of man that I would wed
Would be a rugby fly-half.

And he'd whip it out and I'd whip it out,
We'd both whip it out together,
We'd both be all right in the middle of the night
Whipping it out together.

If I were the marrying kind,
Which I thank the Lord I'm not, Sir,
The kind of man that I would wed
Would be a rugby scrum-half.

And he'd put it in and I'd put it in,
We'd both put it in together,
We'd both be all right in the middle of the night
Putting it in together.

If I were the marrying kind,
Which I thank the Lord I'm not, Sir,
The kind of man that I would wed
Would be a rugby hooker.

And he'd strike hard and I'd strike hard,
We'd both strike hard together,
We'd be all right in the middle of the night
Striking hard together.

If I were the marrying kind,
Which I thank the Lord I'm not, Sir,
The kind of man that I would wed
Would be a big prop-forward.

And he'd bind tight and I'd bind tight,
We'd both bind tight together,
We'd be all right in the middle of the night
Binding tight together.

If I were the marrying kind,
Which I thank the Lord I'm not, Sir,
The kind of man that I would wed
Would be a referee.

And he'd blow hard and I'd blow hard
We'd both blow hard together,
We'd both be all right in the middle of the night
Blowing hard together.

There was a young fellow from Stroud,
Who was fingering his bird in the crowd
A young man at the front
Said (sniff) 'I can smell c**t',
Just like that, very loud.

The Hole in the Elephant's Bottom

My ambition's to go on the stage;
From this you can see that I've got 'em.
In pantomime I'm all the rage,
I'm the hole in the elephant's bottom.

Oh! The girls all think that I'm it,
As they sit in the stalls I can spot 'em,
And I wink at the girls in the pit
Through the hole in the elephant's bottom.

One night we performed in a farce
And they stuffed up the bottom with cotton,
But it split and I showed my bare arse
Through the hole in the elephant's bottom.

There are pockets inside in the cloth
For two bottles of Bass, if you've got 'em,
But they hiss and they boo when I blow out
    the froth
Through the hole in the elephant's bottom.

Now my part hasn't got any words
But there's nothing that can't be forgotten,
I spend all my time pushing property turds
Through the hole in the elephant's bottom.

Some may think that this story is good
And some may believe that it's rotten,
But those that don't like it can stuff it right up
The hole in the elephant's bottom.

Should the Japanese make an attack,
Then hundreds of bombs – they will drop 'em,
But we'll keep 'em at bay with an Oerliken gun
Through the hole in the elephant's bottom.

The Whole World Over

She was poor but she was honest
Victim of a rich man's whim,
First he f**ked her then he left her
And she had a child by him.

CHORUS

It's the same the whole world over,
It's the poor wot gets the blame,
It's the rich wot gets the pleasure
Aint it all a bleedin' shame?

Standing on the bridge at midnight,
Throwing snowballs at the moon,
She said, 'George I've never 'ad it.'
But she spoke too f**kin' soon.

CHORUS

Then she came to London city,
To recover her fair name,
But another bastard f**ked her,
Now she's on the streets again.

CHORUS

Standing on the bridge at midnight,
Cracking walnuts with her crutch,
She said, 'Jack I've never 'ad it.'
He said, 'No? Not f**kin' much!'

CHORUS

See the little country cottage,
Where her simple parents live,
Though they drink the fizz she sends 'em,
On her achin' quim they live.

CHORUS

Now she stands in Piccadilly,
Pickin' blackheads from her quim,
She is now completely ruined,
And it's all because of him.

CHORUS

She got pox and 'orrid chankers,
From the wolves that plumbed her gut,
So she went down to the river,
For to give her whorin' up.

CHORUS

As they pulled her from the water,
Water from her clothes they rung,
And they thought that she had had it,
But the corpse got up and sung.

CHORUS

See him seated in his Bentley,
Coming homeward from the hunt,
He got riches from his marriage,
She got corns upon her c**t.

CHORUS

See him in the House of Commons,
Passing laws for all mankind,
While she walks the streets of London,
Selling chunks of her behind.

CHORUS

The Ball of Kerrimuir

Twas at the gatherin' of the Clans,
And all the Scots were there,
'A feelin' up the lassies
Among the pubic hair.

CHORUS

Singin' balls to your partner
Arse against the wall,
If you can't get f**ked this Saturday night,
You'll never get f**ked at all.

There was f**king in the haystacks,
F**king in the ricks,
You couldn't hear the music,
For the swishin' of the pricks.

CHORUS

The Undertaker he was there,
Dressed in a long black shroud,
Swingin' from a chandelier,
And pissin' on the crowd.

CHORUS

The village cripple he was there,
But didn't shag too much,
His old John Thomas had fallen off
So he f**ked 'em with his crutch.

CHORUS

The local sweepy he was there,
A really filthy brute,
And every time he farted,
He covered 'em all with soot.

CHORUS

The village idiot he was there,
Up to his favourite trick,
Bouncin' on his testicles,
And whistlin' through his prick.

CHORUS

The district nurse was there as well,
She had us all in fits,
Jumping off the mantlepiece,
And landin' on her tits.

CHORUS

The village copper he was there,
He had a mighty tool,
He pulled his foreskin o'er his head,
And yodelled through the hole.

CHORUS

The country postman he was there,
He had a dose of pox,
As he couldn't f**k the lassies,
He stuffed the letter box.

CHORUS

The old fishmonger he was there,
A dirty stinkin' sod,
He never got a stand that night,
So he f**ked 'em with a cod.

CHORUS

The local Vicar he was there,
His collar back to front,
He said, 'My girls thy sins are blest.'
And shoved it up their c**ts.

CHORUS

There was buggery in the parlour,
Sodomy on the stairs,
You couldn't see the dancin' floor,
For the mass of pubic hairs.

CHORUS

There was wee Dr Jameson,
The one that fought the Boers,
He leaped up on the table,
And shouted for the whores.

CHORUS

Jock the blacksmith he was there,
He couldn't play the game,
He f**ked a lassie seven times
And wouldn't see her hame.

CHORUS

The village elders they were there,
And they were shocked to see,
Four and twenty maidenheads,
A hangin' from a tree.

CHORUS

The old schoolmaster he was there,
He f**ked by rule of thumb;
By logarithms he worked out
The time that he would come.

CHORUS

Four and twenty virgins,
Came down from Cuiremore,
Only two came back again,
And they were double bore.

CHORUS

In the morning early,
The farmer nearly shat,
For twenty acres of his corn,
Were fairly f**kin' flat.

CHORUS

And when the ball was over,
The maidens all confessed,
Although they liked the music
The f**king was the best.

CHORUS

In Mobile

Oh the shitehawks they fly high in Mobile,
Oh the shitehawks they fly high in Mobile,
Oh the shitehawks they fly high
And they shit right in your eye,
It's a good things cows can't fly in Mobile.

Oh the old brown cow is dead in Mobile,
Oh the old brown cow is dead in Mobile,
Oh the old brown cow is dead
But the children must be fed
So we'll milk the bull instead in Mobile.

There's a lady they call Susan in Mobile,
There's a lady they call Susan in Mobile,
There's a lady they call Susan
And her c**t she's always usin'
She's got the best infusion in Mobile.

There's a shortage of good whores in Mobile,
There's a shortage of good whores in Mobile,
There's a shortage of good whores
So we'll f**k the shithouse doors,
And there's knotholes in the floors in Mobile.

Oh I knew a parson's daughter in Mobile,
Oh I knew a parson's daughter in Mobile,
Oh I knew a parson's daughter,
Sought her, caught her, f**ked her, taught her,
Now I cannot pass my water in Mobile.

Among the upper classes in Mobile,
Among the upper classes in Mobile,
Among the upper classes,
When they finished with their glasses
They just stuff them up their arses in Mobile.

There's no paper in the bogs in Mobile,
There's no paper in the bogs in Mobile,
There's no paper in the bogs
So we'll shit until it clogs
Then we'll saw it off in logs in Mobile.

The vicar is a bugger in Mobile,
The vicar is a bugger in Mobile,
The vicar is a bugger,
And the verger is another,
And they bugger one another in Mobile.

All the seagulls have a lighthouse in Mobile,
All the seagulls have a lighthouse in Mobile,
All the seagulls have a lighthouse
And they use it as a shitehouse,
Now the lighthouse is a whitehouse in Mobile.

There's a shortage of san(itary) towels in
    Mobile,
There's a shortage of san(itary) towels in
    Mobile,
There's a shortage of san towels,
So they wait until it fouls,
And then dig it out with trowels in Mobile.

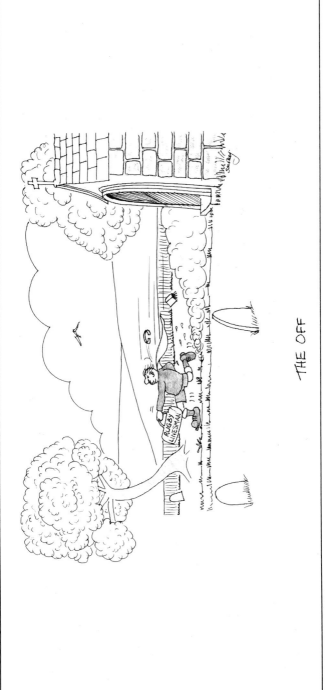

THE OFF

Ernie

You could hear his knackers pound, as he raced
across the ground
And the swishing of his prick, as he swung it round
and round.
He galloped into Market Street, he wore no pants
or vest
His name was Ernie and he had the biggest
chopper in the west.

REFRAIN

Ernie, Ernie — He had the biggest chopper
in the west.

Now Ernie f**ked a widow, a lady known as Sue
She said "I'd like to try it" he said "Yes I bet you
do."
They said she was too big for him she had it twice
a week
But Ernie got his chopper out, and all her flesh
went weak.

REFRAIN

Now Ernie had a rival, an evil f**king man,
Called one-balled Ted from Teddington, who drove
the Durex van.
He tempted her with his Featherlite, till he got his
end away
And all Ernie had to offer was his oats three times a
day.

REFRAIN

One day Ernie saw Ted's van outside the widow's
    door.
It drove him mad to find out it was still there at half
    past four.
Ernie had a bastard on, it really made him sick
So he went and smashed Ted's windows with a
    great big f*****g brick.

REFRAIN

Now Ted he ran out into the street, his eyes upon
    the brick.
They stood there face to face and Ted went for his
    prick.
But Ernie was to quick for him; it wasn't the way
    Ted planned,
And a hairy sweaty bollock, sent it spinning from
    his hand.

REFRAIN

Now Sue she stepped between them, and tried to
    keep them apart.
But Ernie turned and said, "F**k off you silly looking
    tart".
He turned round to face Ted, ready to make his
    thrust
But a size ten spunk ball hit him, and Ernie bit the
    dust.

REFRAIN

Ernie was only 22 he didn't want to die,
And now he shags his arse off, in that brothel in the
    sky.
Where there aren't any virgins, he's f****d them all
    by force
And the clap in his left bollock, goes from bad to
    worse.

REFRAIN

Now a woman's needs are many fold, so Sue she
    slept with Ted
And strange things happened on their wedding
    night, as they lay there in their bed.
Was that the trees a-rustling, or maybe even more,
Like Ernie's ghostly chopper, a banging on the
    door.

They won't forget old Ernie 'cos he had the biggest
    chopper in the west!

There was a young fellow from Bicester
Who wanted to roger his sister.
She said 'It's unlawful,
in fact it's quite awful ,
So she tossed him off while he kissed her.

THE REF.

The Tinker

A beautiful young maiden
Was dressing for the ball,
When she espied a tinker
Wanking off against the wall.

CHORUS

With his great big kidney wiper
And his balls the size of three,
And a yard and a half of foreskin
Hanging down below his knee.

She wrote to him a letter
And in it she did say,
"I'd rather be shagged by you Sir
Than my husband any day."

CHORUS

The tinker got the letter
And when it he did read,
His balls began to fester
And his prick began to bleed.

CHORUS

He mounted on his charger
The castle for to ride,
With his prick high in the saddle
And his balls on either side.

CHORUS

He rode up to the castle
He rode up to the wall
"By golly," said the butler
"He's come to shag us all."

CHORUS

He shagged them in the pantry,
He shagged them in the hall,
But the way he shagged the butler
Was the funniest way of all.

CHORUS

Some say he went to heaven,
Some say he went to hell,
Some say he shagged the devil
I'll bet he shagged him well.

CHORUS

There was a young fellow called Crocket
Went up to space in a rocket.
The rocket went bang,
And his balls went clang,
And he found his cock in his pocket.

The Portions of the Female

The portions of a woman that appeal to man's
    depravity,
Are fashioned with considerable care,
And what at first appears to be a simple little cavity,
Is really an elaborate affair.

Now surgeons who have studied these feminine
    phenomena,
By numerous experiments on Dames,
Have taken all the items of the gentle sex's
    abdomina
And given them delightful Latin names.

There's the Vulva, the Vagina and the good old
    Peronina,
And the Hymen that is sometimes found in brides,
There's a lot of little things − you'd love 'em could
    you see 'em
The Clitoris and God knows what besides.

What a pity it is then, when the common people
    chatter
Of those mysteries to which I have referred,
We use for such a delicate and complicated matter,
Such a very short and unattractive word.

The erudite authorities who study the geography.
Of that obscure but entertaining land,
Are able to indulge a taste for intricate topography,
And view the tasty details close at hand.

But ordinary people though aware of their
    existence,
And complexities beneath the pubic bone,
Are normally contented to view them at a distance,
And treat them as an interesting zone.

And therefore when we laymen probe the secrets
  of virginity,
We exercise a simple sense of touch,
We don't cloud the issue with meticulous Latinity,
But call the whole concern a simple CRUTCH.

For men have made this useful and intelligent
  commodity,
The topic of innumerable jibes,
And though the name they call it by, is something
  of an oddity,
It seems to fit the subject they describe.

There once was a lady called Annie,
Who had fleas, lice, and crabs up her fanny.
To get up her flue
Was like touring the zoo,
There were wild beasts in each nook
  and cranny.

'Zulu Warrior'

Aye zigga-zumba, zumba zumba
Aye zigga-zumba zumba zae
Get' em down you Zulu warrior
Get' em down you Zulu Chief, Chief Chief Chief.

Sing a Song of Syphilis

Sing a song of syphilis,
A foreskin full of crabs.
Four and twenty blackheads
And a score or more of scabs.
And when the scabs were opened
The crabs began to sing.
And wasn't that a dirty thing
To stick up Nellie's quim.

The German Officers

Three German officers crossed the line,
Parlez vous,
Three German officers crossed the line,
Parlez vous,
Three German officers crossed the line
They f****d the women
and drank the wine,
Inky, Pinky, Parlez vous.

as above...

They came upon a wayside inn,
Shat on the mat and walked right in.

Oh landlord have you a daughter fair,
Lily-white tits and golden hair?

At last they got her on the bed,
Shagged her till her cheeks were red.

And then they took her to a shed,
Shagged her till she was nearly dead.

They took her down a shady lane,
Shagged her back to life again.

They shagged her up, they shagged her down,
They shagged her right around the town.

They shagged her in, they shagged her out,
They shagged her up the waterspout.

Seven months went by and all was well,
Eight months went and she started to swell.

Nine months went, she gave a grunt,
A little white bastard popped out of her c**t.

The little white bastard he grew and grew,
He shagged his mother and sister too.

The little white bastard he went to hell,
He shagged the Devil and his wife as well.

An insatiable nymph from Penzance,
Travelled by bus to South Hants.
Five others f**ked her,
Besides the conductor,
And the driver came twice in his pants.

Cats on the Rooftops

When you wake up in the morning
With a devil of a stand,
From the pressure of the liquid
On your seminary gland.
If your wife won't let you,
Damn it you've got a hand,
And you can revel in the joys of masturbation.

CHORUS

Cats on the rooftops.
Cats on the tiles.
Cats with syphilis.
Cats with piles.
Cats with their arseholes
Wreathed in smiles,
As they revel in the joys
Of copulation.

When you wake up in the morning
And you're feeling full of joy,
And your wife's got the rags on
And your daughter's feeling coy,
Then shove it up the bottom
Of your youngest boy,
And revel in the joys of copulation.

CHORUS

Bow-legged women shit like goats,
Bald-headed men all like stoats,
While the congregation sits and gloats
And revels in the joys of copulation.

CHORUS

Now the donkey on the common
Is a disappointed bloke,
He lives for years and doesn't get a poke,
So when he does he lets it soak,
And revels in the joys of copulation.

CHORUS

The orang-utan is a colourful sight
There's a glow on his arse like a pilot light,
As it jumps and it leaps in the night,
As it revels in the joys of copulation.

CHORUS

The giraffe is an animal so it seems
That very rarely has wet dreams,
But when he does he comes in streams,
As he revels in the joys of copulation.

CHORUS

Now I met a girl and she was a dear
But she gave me a dose of gonorrheoa,
Fools rush in where angels fear,
To revel in the joys of copulation.

CHORUS

Do you ken John Peel with his coat so gay,
He's a dirty old sod so all the men say,
For they can't toss off in the usual way,
So his hounds lick his horn in the morning.

CHORUS

Swing Low Sweet Chariot

Swing low sweet chariot
Coming for to carry me home.
Swing low sweet chariot
Coming for to carry me home.

I looked over Jordan and what did I see
Coming for to carry me home,
A band of angels coming after me
Coming for to carry me home.

Swing low sweet chariot
Coming for to carry me home
Swing low sweet chariot
Coming for to carry me home.

That's it!

Nº 9.

Christopher Robin

Little boy sits on the lavatory seat
Little boy's trousers round little boy's feet,
Splish, splash into the pit
Christopher Robin is having a shit.

Little boy stands by the lavatory seat
Little boy's trousers round little boy's feet,
Splish, splash into the tank
Christopher Robin is having a wank.

Little boy stands at the fireside fender
Little boy's fingers round masculine gender,
Phist, Phist into the fire
Christopher Robin is pulling his wire.

Little boy kneels at the side of his pit
Little boy's foreskin all covered in shit,
Hush! Hush! don't tell mother
Christopher Robin has buggered his brother.

Little boy stands at the foot of the stairs
Little boy's hands full of curly black hairs,
F**king great carving knife stuck in the mat
Christopher Robin's castrated the cat.

Old King Cole

Old King Cole was a merry old soul,
And a merry old soul was he.
He called for his wife
In the middle of the night,
And he called for his fiddlers three.
Now every fiddler had a very fine fiddle,
And a very fine fiddle had he.
Fiddle diddle dee, diddle dee,
Said the fiddlers,
What merry men are we.
There's none so fair as can compare,
As the boys of the R.F.C.

Old King Cole was a merry old soul,
And a merry old soul was he.
He called for his wife
In the middle of the night,
And he called for his tailors three.
Now every tailor had a very fine needle,
And a very fine needle had he.
Stick it in and out, in and out,
Said the tailors.
Fiddle diddle dee, diddle dee,
Said the fiddlers,
What merry men are we.
There's none so fair as can compare,
With the boys of the R.F.C.

Old King Cole was a merry old soul,
And a merry old soul was he.
He called for his wife
In the middle of the night,
And he called for his jugglers three.
Now every juggler
Had two very fine balls,
And two very fine balls had he.
Throw your balls in the air,
Said the jugglers.
Stick it in and out, in and out,
Said the tailors.
Fiddle diddle dee, diddle dee,
Said the fiddlers.
What merry men are we.
There's none so fair as can compare
With the boys of the R.F.C.

Slap it up and down, up and down,
Said the painter.
Lay your meat on the block,
Said the butcher.
I've got a horn, got a horn,
Said the huntsman.
Will you have it in the back or the front?,
Said the coalman.
I've got crabs, got crabs
Said the fisherman.
I've got a dose, got a dose,
Said the chemist.
Push it up your pipe, up your pipe,
Said the plumber.
May our Lord save our souls from damnation,
Said the parson.

A Christmas Carol

On the first day of Christmas
My true love sent to me My Lord Montague of
Burleigh.

On the second day of Christmas
My true love sent to me two girl guides and my
Lord Montague of Burleigh.

On the third day of Christmas
My true love sent to me three boy scouts, two girl
guides and my Lord Montague of Burleigh.

On the fourth day of Christmas
My true love sent to me four choir boys, three boy
scouts, two girl guides, and my Lord Montague of
Burleigh.

On the fifth day of Christmas
My true love sent to me five windmill girls, four
choir boys, three boy scouts, two girl guides and
my Lord Montague of Burleigh.

On the sixth day of Christmas
My true love sent to me six convicted vicars, five
windmill girls, four choir boys, three boy scouts,
two girl guides and my Lord Montague of
Burleigh.

On the seventh day of Christmas
My true love sent to me seven sex starved
spinsters, six convicted vicars, five windmill girls,
four choir boys, three boy scouts, two girl guides
and my Lord Montague of Burleigh.

On the eighth day of Christmas
My true love sent to me eight useless eunuchs,
   seven sex starved spinsters, six convicted vicars,
   five windmill girls, four choir boys three boy
   scouts, two girl guides and my Lord Montague of
   Burleigh.

On the ninth day of Christmas
My true love sent to me nine naughty nancies,
   eight useless eunuchs, seven sex starved
   spinsters, six convicted vicars, five windmill girls,
   four choir boys, three boy scouts, two girl guides
   and my Lord Montague of Burleigh.

On the tenth day of Christmas
My true love sent to me ten turkish tarts, nine
   naughty nancies, eight useless eunuchs, seven
   sex starved spinsters, six convicted vicars, five
   windmill girls, four choir boys three boy scouts,
   two girl guides And my Lord Montague of
   Burleigh.

On the eleventh day of Christmas
My true love sent to me eleven lecherous lesbians,
   ten turkish tarts, nine naughty nancies, eight
   useless eunuchs, seven sex starved spinsters,
   six convicted vicars, five windmill girls, four choir
   boys, three boy scouts, two girl guides and my
   Lord Montague of Burleigh.

On the twelfth day of Christmas
My true love sent to me twelve twisted titties,
   eleven lecherous lesbians, ten turkish tarts, nine
   naughty nancies, eight useless eunuchs, seven
   sex starved spinsters, six convicted vicars, five
   windmill girls, four choir boys, three boy scouts,
   two girl guides And my Lord Montague of
   Burleigh.

The Mayor's Daughter

The Mayor of Bayswater has got a lovely daughter
And the hairs on her dicky di do hang down to her
knees.

CHORUS

One black one, one white one and one with
a bit of shite on,
And the hairs on her dicky di do hang down
to her knees.

If she were my daughter I'd have them cut shorter,
And the hairs on her dicky di do hang down to her
knees.

CHORUS

I've smelt it, I've felt it, it's just like a bit of velvet,
And the hairs on her dicky di do hang down to her
knees.

CHORUS

I've seen it, I've seen it, I've been in between it,
And the hairs on her dicky di do hang down to her
knees.

CHORUS

It would take a coal miner to find her vagina,
And the hairs on her dicky di do hang down to her
knees.

CHORUS

She married an Italian with balls like a bloody
  stallion,
And the hairs on her dicky di do hang down to her
  knees.

CHORUS

She lived in a lighthouse which was more like a
  f**king shitehouse,
And the hairs on her dicky di do hang down to her
  knees.

CHORUS

Her mum came from Glamorgan and had a c**t like
  a barrel organ,
And the hairs on her dicky di do hang down to her
  knees.

CHORUS

She slept with a demon who washed her with
  semen,
And her hairs on her dicky di do hang down to her
  knees.

CHORUS

Oh Sir Jasper

She wears her silk pyjamas in the summer when
   it's hot.
She wears her woollen nighty in the winter when
   it's not.
But sometimes in the springtime and sometimes in
   the fall,
She slips between the sheets with nothing on at all.

She's a most immoral lady,
She's a most immoral lady,
She's a most immoral lady,
And she lay between the sheets with nothing on at
   all.

REPEAT 1ST VERSE

Oh Sir Jasper do not touch me,
Oh Sir Jasper do not touch me,
Oh Sir Jasper do not touch me,
And she lay between the sheets with nothing on at
   all.

REPEAT 1ST VERSE

Glory, Glory Hallelujah,
See the devil coming to yuh,
He's gonna put his prick right through yuh
For jumping into bed with nothing on at all.

REPEAT LAST VERSE

THE
SKIPPER

Eskimo Nell

When a man grows old and his balls grow cold and
   the end of his nob turns blue,
When it's bent in the middle like a one string fiddle,
   he can tell a yarn or two.

So find me a seat and stand me a drink and a tale
   to you I'll tell,
Of Dead-Eye Dick and Mexico Pete and the gentle
   Eskimo Nell.

Now when Dead-Eye Dick and Mexico Pete go
   forth in search of fun,
It's usually Dick who wields the prick and Mexico
   Pete the gun.

And when Dead-Eye Dick and Mexico Pete are
   sore, depressed and mad,
'Tis a c**t that generally bears the brunt – so the
   shootin·'aint too bad.

Now Dead-Eye Dick and Mexico Pete had been
   hunting in dead man's creek,
And they'd had no luck in the way of a f**k for nigh
   on half a week.

Just a moose or two or a caribou and a bison-cow
   or so,
And for Dead-Eye Dick and his kingly prick this
   f**king was mighty slow.

So do or dare this horny pair set out for the Rio
   Grande,
Dead-Eye Dick with his muscular prick and Pete
   with his gun in hand.

And as they blazed their randy trail, no man in their
   path withstood,
And many a bride who was hubby's pride knew
   pregnant widowhood.

They made the strand of Rio Grande at the height
 of a blazing noon,
And to slake their thirst and do their worst they
 sought Black Mike's saloon.

As the swing doors opened wide, both prick and
 gun flashed free,
'Accordin' to sex, you bleedin' wrecks, you drinks
 or f**ks with me!'

Now they'd heard of the prick called Dead-Eye Dick
 from the Horn to Panama,
And with nothing worse than a muttered curse
 those cowhands sought the bar.

The women too knew his playful ways down on the
 Rio Grande,
And forty whores took down their drawers at Dead-
 Eye Dicks command.

They saw the fingers of Mexico Pete twitch on the
 trigger grip.
'Twas death to wait and at a fearful rate those
 whores began to strip.

Now Dead-Eye Dick was breathing quick with
 lecherous snorts and grunts,
As forty arses were bared to view to say nothing of
 forty c**ts!

Now forty arses and forty c**ts you'll see if you use
 your wits,
And rattle a bit at arithmetic – that's likewise eighty
 tits.

And eighty tits is a gladsome sight for a man with a
 raging stand,
They may be rare in Berkeley Square, but not on
 the Rio Grande.

Our Dead-Eye Dick he f**ks 'em quick, so he
  backed and took a run,
He made a dart at the nearest tart and scored a
  bull in one,

He bore her to the sandy floor and f**ked her deep
  and fine,
And though she grinned it put the wind up the other
  thirty nine.

Our Dead-Eye Dick, he f**ks 'em quick, and flinging
  the first aside,
He was making a grin at the second quim when the
  swing doors opened wide.

And into that hall of sin and vice – into that harlot's
  hell,
Strode a gentle maid who was unafraid, her name
  was Eskimo Nell.

Our Dead-Eye Dick who f**ks 'em quick was well
  into number twenty two,
When Eskimo Nell lets out a yell and says to him,
  'Hey-you.'

The hefty lout he turned about, both nob and face
  were red,
With a single flick of his mighty prick the tart flew
  over his head.

But Eskimo Nell she stood it well and looked him in
  the eyes,
With the utmost scorn she glimpsed the horn that
  rose from his hairy thighs.

She blew a puff from her cigarette onto his
  steaming nob,
So utterly beat was Mexico Pete he forgot to do his
  job.

It was Eskimo Nell who broke the spell in accents
    calm and cool,
'You c**t-struck shrimp of a Yankee pimp, do you
    call that thing a tool?'

'If this here town can't take that down', she
    sneered
    to the cowering whores,
'There's one little c**t that can do the stunt – it's
    Eskimo Nell's not yours.'

She shed her garments one by one with an air of
    conscious pride,
Till at last she stood in her womanhood, and they
    saw the great divide.

She laid right down on a table top where someone
    had left a glass,
With a twitch of her tits she crushed it to bits
    between the cheeks of her arse!

She bent her knees with supple ease and opened
    her legs apart;
With a final nod to the randy sod she gave him the
    cue to start.

But Dead-Eye Dick with his king of a prick prepared
    to take his time,
For a girl like this was a f**king bliss – so he staged
    a pantomime.

He winked his arsehole in and out, and made his
    balls inflate,
Until they looked like granite knobs on top of a
    garden gate.

He rubbed his foreskin up and down-his nob
    increased in size,
His mighty prick grew twice as thick and almost
    reached his eyes.

He polished his rod with Rum and gob to make it
steaming hot,
And to finish the job he sprinkled the nob with a
cayenne pepper pot.

He didn't back to take a run, nor yet a flying leap,
But bent right down and came longside with a
steady forward creep.

Then he took sight as a gunman might along his
mighty tool,
And shoved his lust with a dexterous thrust – firm,
calculating and cool.

Have you seen the massive pistons on the giant
C.P.R.?
With a punishing force of a thousand horses – you
know what pistons are.

Or you think you do, but you've yet to learn the
awe-inspiring trick,
Of the work that's done on a non-stop run by a man
like Dead-Eye Dick.

But Eskimo Nell was an infidel – she equalled a
whole harem,
With the strength of ten in her abdomen and her
rock of ages beam.

Amidships she could stand the rush like the flush of
a water closet,
So she grasped his cock like a Chatwood lock on
the National Safe Deposit.

She lay for a while with a subtle smile while the grip
of her c**t grew keener,
Then giving a sigh she sucked him dry with the
ease of a vacuum cleaner.

She performed this feat in a way so neat as to set
   at complete defiance,
The primary cause and the basic laws that govern
   sexual science.

She calmly rode through the phallic code which for
   years had stood the test,
And the ancient laws of the classic school in a
   moment or two went west.

And now my friend we draw to the end of this
   copulating epic,
The effect on Dick was sudden and quick and akin
   to an anaesthetic.

He slipped on the floor and he knew no more – his
   passions extinct and dead,
He didn't shout as his tool came out; it was stripped
   down to a thread.

Mexico Pete, he sprang to his feet, to avenge his
   pals affront,
With a fearful jolt he drew his Colt and rammed it
   up her c**t.

He shoved it up to the trigger grip and fired three
   times three,
But to his surprise she rolled her eyes and smiled in
   ecstasy.

She leaped to her feet with a smile so sweet,
   'Bully', she said, 'for you.'
'Though I might of guessed it's about the best you
   phoney lechers do'.

'When next your friend and you intend to sally forth
   for fun,
Buy Dead-Eye Dick a sugar stick, and get yourself
   a bun.'

'I'm going back to the frozen North, to the land
 where spunk is spunk,
Not a trickling stream of luke warm cream-but a
 solid frozen chunk.

Back to the land where they understand what it
 means to fornicate,
Where even the dead sleep two in a bed and the
 infants copulate.

Back to the land of the mighty stand,where the
 nights are six months long,
Where the polar bear wanks off in his lair-thats
 where they'll sing this song.

They'll tell this tale on the Arctic trail where the
 nights are sixty below,
Where it's so damned cold, French letters are sold
 wrapped in a ball of snow.

In the valley of death with baited breath it's there
 we sing it too,
Where the skeletons rattle in sexual battle and the
 mouldering corpses screw!'

So Dead-Eye Dick and Mexico Pete slunk out of
 the Rio Grande,
Dead-Eye Dick with his useless prick and Pete with
 no gun in his hand.

When a man grows old and his balls go cold and
 the end of his nob turns blue,
And the hole in the middle refuses to piddle, I'd say
 he was f****d wouldn't you?

Did You Ever See?

Oh, I've got an Aunty Sissy,
And she's only got one titty,
But it's very long and pointed,
And the nipples double jointed.

CHORUS

Did you ever see,
Did you ever see,
Did you ever see,
Such a funny thing before.

I've got a cousin Daniel,
And he's got a cocker spaniel,
If you tickled him in the middle,
He would lift his leg and piddle.

CHORUS

Oh, I've got a cousin Larry,
He plays on the wing for Barry,
They think so much about him,
That they always play without him.

CHORUS

Oh, I've got a cousin Anna,
And she's got a grand piana,
And she ram aram arama,
Till the neighbours say 'God Damn Her.'

CHORUS

The Engineer's Dream

An engineer told me before he died
– Ah rum titty bum, titty bum, titty bum.
An engineer told me before he died
And I've no reason to believe he lied.
– Ah rum titty bum, titty bum, titty bum.
– Ah rum titty bum, titty bum, titty bum
He knew a woman with a c**t so wide.
– Ah rum titty bum, titty bum, titty bum.
He knew a woman with a c**t so wide
That she was never satisfied.
– Ah rum titty bum, titty bum, titty bum
– Ah rum titty bum, titty bum, titty bum.

So he built a huge great prick of steel
– Ah rum titty bum, titty bum, titty bum.
So he built a huge great prick of steel
Driven by a bloody great wheel.
– Ah rum titty bum, titty bum, titty bum.
– Ah rum titty bum, titty bum, titty bum.
Two brass balls he filled with cream.
– Ah rum titty bum, titty bum, titty bum
Two brass balls he filled with cream
And the whole bloody issue was driven by steam.
– Ah rum titty bum, titty bum, titty bum,
– Ah rum titty bum, titty bum, titty bum.

Round and round went the bloody great wheel
– Ah rum titty bum, titty bum, titty bum.
Round and round went the bloody great wheel
In and out went the prick of steel.
– Ah rum titty bum, titty bum, titty bum.
– Ah rum titty bum, titty bum, titty bum.
Till at last the maiden cried,
– Ah rum titty bum, titty bum, titty bum.
Till at last the maiden cried
'Enough, enough, I'm satisfied.'
– Ah rum titty bum, titty bum, titty bum
– Ah rum titty bum, titty bum, titty bum.

Up and up went the level of steam
– Ah rum titty bum, titty bum, titty bum
Up and up went the level of steam
Down and down went the level of cream.
– Ah rum titty bum, titty bum, titty bum.
– Ah rum titty bum, titty bum, titty bum.
'Til again the maiden cried
– Ah rum titty bum, titty bum, titty bum
'Til again the maiden cried
'Enough,enough, I'm satisfied.'
– Ah rum titty bum, titty bum, titty bum
– Ah rum titty bum, titty bum, titty bum.

Now we come to the tragic bit
– Ah rum titty bum, titty bum, titty bum
Now we come to the tragic bit
There was no way of stopping it.
– Ah rum titty bum, titty bum, titty bum.
– Ah rum titty bum, titty bum, titty bum.
She was split from arse to tit
– Ah rum titty bum, titty bum, titty bum.
She was split from arse to tit
And the whole bloody issue was covered in shit.
– Ah rum titty bum, titty bum, titty bum
– Ah rum titty bum, titty bum, titty bum.

Nº 8.

Ou est le Papier?

A Frenchman went to the lavatory
To enjoy a jolly good shit.
He took his coat and trousers off
So that he could revel in it.
But when he reached for the paper,
He found that someone had been there before,
    'Ou est le papier?'
    'Ou est le papier?'
'Bonjour Monsieur, je fait manure,
    Ou est le papier?'

There was a young man from Nantucket,
Whose cock was so long he could suck it.
He said with a grin
As he wiped off his chin,
'If my ear was a c**t, I could f**k it.'

Will You Marry Me?

If I give you half-a-crown
Can I take your knickers down,
Will you marry, marry marry marry,
Will you marry me?

If you give me half-a-crown
You can't take my knickers down,
You can't marry, marry marry marry,
You can't marry me.

If I give you fish and chips
Will you let me squeeze your tits,
Will you marry, marry marry marry,
Will you marry me?

If you give me fish and chips
I won't let you squeeze my tits,
You can't marry, marry marry marry,
You can't marry me.

If I give you my big chest
And all the money I possess,
Will you marry, marry marry marry,
Will you marry me?

If you give me your big chest
And all the money you possess,
I will marry, marry marry marry,
I will marry you.

Get out the door, you lousy whore,
My money was all you were looking for,
And I'll not marry, marry marry marry,
I'll not marry you.

Ring the Bell Verger

CHORUS

Ring the bell, verger, ring the bell ring,
Perhaps the congregation will condescend
to sing,
Perhaps the organist sitting on his stool,
Will play upon the organ and not upon his tool.

Down in the jungle director sits,
Playing with the lady producer's tits.
Announcers voice comes from miles and miles,
Stop twiddling tits and twiddle dials.

CHORUS

Handsome butler, buxom cook,
Down in the pantry having a f**k,
Mistress' voice is heard in appeal,
'Stop f**king cook, cook f**king meal'.

CHORUS

In the garage chauffeur lies,
Vicars wife between his thighs,
Vicar's voice is heard from afar,
'Stop f**king wife and start the f**king car.'

CHORUS

Down in the beach hut Lord Montague lies,
3 or 4 Boy scouts stuck like flies,
Neptune's voice a'comes from the sea,
Wipe their f**king arseholes and pass them on
to me.

CHORUS

Ocean liner arriving late,
Dirty stoker poking mate,
Frantic message, urgent wires,
'Stop poking mate and start poking fires'.

CHORUS

In the choir stalls, choir boys sing,
Praises to our heavenly king,
Choir master sits, twiddling his thumbs,
Contemplating choir boys bums.

CHORUS

In the belfry verger stands,
Pulling on his pulley with his bloody great hands,
Vicar's voice is heard in appeal,
'Stop pulling pud and start pulling peal'.

There was a young man of St James,
Who indulged in the jolliest games.
He lighted the rim
Of his grandmother's quim,
And laughed as she pissed through
   the flames.

The Good Ship Venus

'Twas on the good ship Venus,
By Christ you should have seen us;
The figure-head was a whore in bed,
And the mast was a rampant penis.

CHORUS

Frigging in the rigging,
Wanking on the planking,
Masturbating on the grating
There was f**k all else to do.

The captain of this lugger
He was a filthy bugger,
Declared unfit to shovel shit
From one ship to another.

CHORUS

The cabin-boy called Dripper,
Was a foul-mouthed little nipper,
Who stuffed his arse with broken glass
To circumcise the skipper.

CHORUS

The first mate's name was Morgan,
A veritable gorgon;
Each night at eight, he'd play till late
Upon his extra-sexual organ.

CHORUS

The boatswain was named Andy
A Portsmouth man and randy,
His whopping cock broke chunks of rock,
To cool the skipper's brandy.

CHORUS

His wife was baptised Charlotte,
Who was born and bred a harlot,
At night her c**t was lily-white,
In the morning it was scarlet.

CHORUS

The captain's daughter Mabel,
Though young was fresh and able,
To suck and shake and fornicate,
Upon the chart-room table.

CHORUS

His other little daughter,
Got shoved into the water,
Her plaintive squeals announced that eels,
Had found her sexual quarters.

CHORUS

The ships dog was called Rover,
We turned the poor thing over,
And ground and ground that faithful hound,
From Tenerife to Dover.

CHORUS

Through skilful navigation,
We reached our China station.
We sunk a junk on a sea of spunk,
Through mutual masturbation.

CHORUS

There was a Rabbi named Keith
Who circumcised men with his teeth.
It was not for the treasure,
Nor sexual pleasure,
But to get to the cheese underneath.

F**k 'em All

F**k 'em all, f**k 'em all,
The long and the short and the tall,
F**k all the blonde c**ts and all the brunettes,
Don't be too choosy, just f**k all you gets,
'Cause we're saying goodbye to them all,
As back to the barracks we crawl,
You'll get no erection at short-arm inspection,
So pack up you men, f**k 'em all.

F**k 'em all, f**k 'em all,
The long and the short and the tall,
F**k all the c**ts 'til you break them in two,
You'll get no loving where you're going to,
'Cause we're saying goodbye to them all,
As back to the barracks we crawl,
So get your big prick up and give it a stick up,
Cheer up my lads, f**k 'em all.

There was a lady from Thorey,
Who went for a piss in a quarry.
She laid on her back
And opened her crack,
And Harry backed in with his lorry.

FRONT ROW MAN

The Virgin Sturgeon

Caviar comes from the virgin sturgeon,
Virgin Sturgeon very fine dish.
Virgin Sturgeon needs no urgin',
That's why Caviar is my dish.

Shad roe comes from scarlet Shad Fish,
Shad Fish have a sorry fate.
Pregnant Shad Fish is a sad fish,
Got that way without a mate.

Oysters, they are fishy bivalves,
They have youngsters in their shells,
How they diddle is a riddle,
But they do, so what the hell.

The green sea Turtle's mate is happy,
With her lover's winning ways.
First he grips her with his flippers,
Then he grips and flips for days.

I fed caviar to my girl friend,
She's a virgin, tried and true.
Now that virgin, needs no urgin'
There ain't nothing she won't do.

Mrs Clam is optimistic,
Shoots her eggs out in the sea.
Hopes her suitor is a shooter,
Hits the self-same spot as she.

Give a thought to a happy Cod Fish,
Always there when duty calls,
Female Cod Fish is an odd fish,
From them too come cod fish balls.

The Trout is just a little Salmon,
Just half grown and minus scales,
But the Trout, just like the Salmon,
Can't get on without its tail.

Lucky fishes are the Ray fish,
When for youngsters they essay,
Yes, my hearties, they have parties,
In the good old fashioned way.

There was a young lady from Itching,
Sat scratching her nose in the kitchen,
Her mother said, 'Rose,
It's pox I suppose',
She said 'Bollocks, get on with
    your knitting.'

Bye, Bye, Blackbird

Once a boy was no good,
Took a girl into a wood.
Bye, bye, Blackbird.
Laid her down upon the grass,
Pinched her tits and slapped her arse.
Bye, bye, Blackbird.
Took her where nobody else could find her,
To a place where he could really grind her.
Rolled her over on her front,
Shoved his cock right up her c**t.
Blackbird, bye, bye.

But this girl was no sport,
Took her story to a court,
Bye, bye, Blackbird.
Told her story in the morn,
All the jury had the horn.
Bye, bye blackbird.
Then the judge came to his decision,
This poor sod got eighteen months in prison,
So next time, boy, do it right,
Stuff her c**t with dynamite,
Blackbird, bye, bye.

The Hedgehog Song

Recent extensive researches,
By Darwin, Huxley and Ball,
Have conclusively proved that the hedgehog,
Has never been buggered at all.

CHORUS

Sing Torrel-i-orrel-i-orrel
Sing Torrel-i-orrel-i-aye,
Sing Torrel-i-orrel-i-orrel
Sing Torrel-i-orrel-i-aye.

Further experimentations,
Have incontrovertibly shown,
That comparative safety at Harvard,
Is enjoyed by the hedgehog alone.

CHORUS

In the process of syphilisation,
From anthropoid ape down to man,
The palm is awarded to Harvard,
For buggering whatever it can.

CHORUS

This rough little, tough little bastard,
Has got prickles all over his arse,
But the students of Yale have now mastered,
A method of slipping it past.

CHORUS

Now why don't they do down at Harvard,
What they finally learnt up at Yale,
And get over this difficult problem,
By shaving the hairs of its tail.

CHORUS

A Clean Story

There was an old sailor who sat on a rock,
Waving his fists and abusing his

Neighbouring farmer watching his ricks,
Teaching his children to play with their

Kites and marbles as in days of yore,
When along came a woman who looked like a

Decent young lady and walked like a duck,
She said she was learning a new way to

Bring up her children and teach them to knit,
While the boys in the farmyard were shovelling

The contents of the pigsty, the muck and the mud,
The squire of the manor was pulling his

Horse from its stable to go to the hunt
His wife in her boudoir was powdering her

Nose and arranging her vanity box
And taking precautions to ward off the

Gout and rheumatics which made her feel stiff
For well did she remember her last dose of

What do you think I was going to say?
No, you rude bugger, that's all for today.

THE SUBSTITUTE.

The Old Apple Tree

In the shade of the old apple tree,
A pair of fine legs I did see,
With some hairs at the top,
And a little red spot,
It looked like a cherry to me.

I pulled out my pride of New York,
It filled it just like a cork;
I said, 'Darlin' don't scream,
While I dish out the cream
In the shade of the old apple tree.'

And as we both lay on the grass,
With my two hands round her fat arse
She said 'If you'll be true,
You can have a suck too!'
In the shade of the old apple tree.

The Bastard King of England

The minstrels sing of a bastard King
Of a thousand years ago,
Who ruled this land with an iron hand
Though his mind was mean and low.

He was very fond of hunting
And roving the Royal wood,
He was also fond of apple-jack
And pulling the Royal pud.

He was forty, fat and full of fleas,
The royal nob hung next to his knees
Twelve inches long and a two inch span,
As King he made a dirty old man.

Now the Queen of Spain was an amorous dame,
And a sprightly wench was she;
She longed to fool with the Royal tool
Of the King across the sea.

So she sent a secret message
By a lean ambassador,
To ask the King if he would spend
A month in bed with her.

Now Phillip of France when he heard this chance,
Within his Royal court,
He swore 'By God, she loves this slob,
Because my tool is short!'

So he sent the rotten Duc d'Alsace
To give the Queen a dose of clap,
To ruin the length and burn the sap
Of the bastard King of England.

When news of this foul deed was heard,
Within fair London's walls,
The King he swore by the Royal whore
He'd have King Phillip's balls.

And he issued a proclamation,
That a tuft of the Queen's c**t hair
He'd give to the sod who brought him the rod,
And the nuts of Phillip the fair.

The brave young Duke of Buckingham
Went instantly to France,
And lay that night with the Royal catamite
And when he downed his pants,

He fastened a thong to fair Phillip's dong
Jumped on a horse and galloped along,
Over the cliffs and under the seas
And brought them both to the Bastard's knees.

Now all the whores in silken drawers,
Sat on the castle walls,
When the Duke sang 'King, I got this thing!'
They merely answered 'Balls'.

But the King threw up his breakfast,
And grovelled on the floor,
For in the ride the French King's pride,
Had stretched a yard or more.

And Phillip alone usurped his throne,
His sceptre was his Royal bone,
He f**ked each member of the Realm,
And the Bastard King went down to hell.

The Great Plenipotentiary

The Bey of Algiers when afraid for his ears,
A messenger sent to our court, Sir;
As he knew in our State that the women have
    weight,
He chose one well hung for good sport, Sir;
He searched the Divan till he found out a man,
Whose bollocks were heavy and hairy,
And he lately came o'er from the Barbary Shore,
As the Great Plenipotentiary.

When to England he came with his prick all aflame,
And showed to his hostess on landing,
Whence spread its renown to all parts of the town,
As a pintle past all understanding.
So much there was said of its snout and its head,
They called it the great Janissary,
Not a Lady could sleep till she got a shy peep
At the Great Plenipotentiary.

As he rode in his coach how the whores did
    approach,
And they stared as if stretched on a tenter;
He drew every eye of the dames that passed by,
Like the wonderful sun to its centre.
As he passed through the town not a window was
    down,
And the maids hurried out just to see;
And the children cried, 'Look – at the man with the
    cock,
That's the Great Plenipotentiary.'

When he came to the Court, O what giggle and
    sport!
Such squinting and squeezing to view him!
What envy and spleen in the women were seen,
Of the happy and pleased that got to him.
They vowed in their hearts, if men of such parts
Were found in the coast of Barbary
'Twas a shame not to bring a whole guard for the
    King,
Like the Great Plenipotentiary.

The dames of intrigue formed their c**ts in a
    league,
To take him in turn the good folk, Sirs;
The young Misses' plan was to catch as catch can,
And all were resolved on a stroke, Sirs!
The cards to invite flew by thousands each night,
With bribes to his old Secretary,
And the famous Eclipse was not let for more leaps,
Than the Great Plenipotentiary.

When his name was announced how the women all
    bounced,
And the blood hurried up to their faces;
He made them all itch from the nave to the breech,
And their bubbies burst out of their laces.
There was such dammed work to be f**ked by the
    Turk,
That nothing their passion could vary;
The whole Nation fell sick for the Tripoli prick
Of the Great Plenipotentiary.

The Duchess who's Duke made her ready to puke
With fumbling and friggin' all night, Sir,
Being first with the prize was so pleased by it size,
That she begged to examine its plight, Sir!
'Good, God', cried Her Grace, 'Its head's like a
mace!
Tis as big as a Corsican Fairy!
I'll make up – please the pigs – for dry-bobs and
frigs,
With the Great Plenipotentiary.'

And now to be bored by this Ottoman Lord,
Came a virgin far gone in the wane, Sir;
She resolved for to try, though her c**t was so dry,
That she knew it must split like a cane, Sir!
True it was as she spoke – it gave way at each
stroke,
But O what a terrible quandary.
With one mighty thrust her old piss-bladder bust
On the Great Plenipotentiary.

The next to be tried was an Alderman's bride,
With a c**t that would swallow a turtle,
Who had horned the dull brows of her worshipful
spouse,
Till they sprouted like Venus's myrtle.
Through thick and through thin, bowel deep he
dashed in,
Till her quim frothed like cream in a dairy,
And expressed by loud farts she was strained in all
parts
By the Great Plenipotentiary.

The next to be kissed by the Plenipo's lift
Was a delicate maiden of honour,
She screamed at the sight of his prick in a fright,
Though she had the whole place upon her;
'C**t Jesus,' she said, 'what a prick for a maid,
Do pray come and look at it Mary.'
Then she cried with a grunt, 'O he's ruined my c**t
With his Great Plenipotentiary!'

Two sisters next came – Peg and Mary by name,
Two ladies of very high breeding,
Resolved one should try whilst the other stood by
To assist in the bloody proceeding:
Peg swore by her God that the Musselman's nob,
Was thick as the buttocks of Mary,
'But I'll have one drive if I'm ripped up alive
By the Great Plenipotentiary.'

All twats were bewitched and just longed to be
    stitched,
Even fairies would languish and linger,
And the boarding school Miss as she sat down to
    piss
Drew a Turk on the floor with her finger.
By fancy so struck they clubbed round for a f**k,
And bought a huge candle and hairy,
And the teachers from France they f**ked a
    distance,
With the Great Plenipotentiary.

Each sluice c**ted bawd who was knocked all
    abroad,
Till her premises gaped like a grave, Sir,
Hoped her luck was on, so she'd feel the Turk's
    dong,
As all others were lost in her cave, Sir.
The nymphs of the stage his fine parts did engage,
Made him free of the grand feminary,
And gentle Signors opened all their black doors
To the Great Plenipotentiary.

Oh love's sweet reward measured out by the yard,
The Turk was most blest of mankind, Sir,
For his powerful dart went home to the heart,
Whether stuck in before or behind, Sir.
But no pencil can draw this long donged Pawshaw,
Thank each c**t loving contemporary,
But as pricks of the game let's drink health to the
    name
Of the Great Plenipotentiary!

There was a young fella named Dave,
Who found a dead whore in a grave.
It took him some pluck
to have a cold f**k,
But look at the money he saved.

Poor Little Angeline

She was sweet sixteen, Little Angeline,
Always playing on the village green,
Never had a thrill, was a virgin still,
    Poor Little Angeline

Now the local Squire got a low desire,
The biggest bastard in the whole damn Shire,
And he set his heart on the vital part
    Of Poor Little Angeline.

Came the village fair, and the Squire was there,
Masturbating in the village square,
When he chanced to see the comely knee
    Of Poor Little Angeline.

As he raised his cap, he said, 'Miss, your cat
has been run over and is squashed quite flat.
My car's in the square, so I'll take you there.'
    My Poor Little Angeline.

They had not gone far when he stopped the car,
And dragged the maiden to the Public Bar,
With a load of gin she would fear no sin,
    Poor Little Angeline.

Now the dirty old turd should have got the bird,
Instead she followed him without a word.
As they drove away you could them say,
    'Poor Little Angeline.'

He had oiled her well, got her in a dell,
And there decided that he'd give her hell,
So he tried his luck with a dog-like f**k,
    At Poor Little Angeline.

Angeline cried, 'Rape', as he raised her cape,
Unhappy darlin' there was no escape,
'Twas time someone came to save the name
    Of Poor Little Angeline.

Now it can he told that the blacksmith bold,
Had loved Little Angeline from time untold,
He was handsome, true and virile too,
    Poor Little Angeline.

But sad to say on that self-same day,
The blacksmith had been put in gaol to stay,
For coming in his pants at the village dance
    With Poor Little Angeline.

Now the bars of the cell overlooked the dell,
Where the Squire was trying to give the
  maiden hell,
As they reached the grass, he saw the arse
    Of his Poor Little Angeline.

So he gave a start and let out a fart,
Strong enough to blow the bars apart,
And he ran like shit, 'cause the Squire might split
    Poor Little Angeline.

When he reached the spot and he saw what's
  what,
He tied the villain's penis in a grannie knot,
And he kicked his guts, bruised the poor sod's
  nuts,
    Poor Little Angeline.

'Blacksmith I love you – Oh indeed I do,
I can see by your trousers that you love me too!
As I am undressed – come and try your best
　　　For Poor Little Angeline.

Now it would be wrong here to end this song,
For the blacksmith had a dong one foot long,
And his natural charm was as thick as your arm,
　　　Lucky Little Angeline.

There was a young girl from Cape Cod,
Who thought that all babies came from God.
It wasn't the Almighty
that went up her nightie,
It was Roger, the lodger, the sod.

THE SCRUM

Sergeant Boon

Hear us sing of Sergeant Boon,
Who used to sleep in the afternoon,

    So tired was he,
    So tired was he.

Down in the woods he used to go,
To doze away an hour or so.

    Down came a bee,
    Busy little bumble-bee.
    Bzz, bzz, bzz, bzz,
    Busy bee, busy bee.

'Get away you bumble bee,
   I ain't no rose;
I ain't no syphilitic bastard,
   Get off my f**kin' nose.
Get off my nasal organ,
   Don't you come near,
If you wanta bit o' fanny
   You can f**k my Granny,
But you'll get no arsehole here.'

    Arsehole rules the Navy,
    Arsehole rules the sea:
    If you wanta bit o' bum,
    You can f**k my chum,
    But you'll get no arse from me!

Aubade for the Shithouse

Come away my love with me
To the public lavatory.

There is an expert there who can,
Encircle thrice the glittering pan.

He, happy youth, has no idea
What suffers from diarrhoea.

Expelling clouds of noisome vapours
Spend annually on toilet papers.

But tranquilly pursues his art,
Or rocks the building with a fart.

O come away my love with me,
To the public lavatory.

There was a young nun from Siberia,
Endowed with a virgin interior.
Until an old monk
Jumped into her bunk,
And now she's the Mother Superior.

Why Beer is Better than Women

1. You can enjoy beer all month.

2. A beer doesn't get jealous when you grab another beer.

3. When you go to a bar you can always pick up another beer.

4. A beer won't get upset if you come home with beer on your breath.

5. You can have more than one beer in a night and not feel guilty.

6. A beer always goes down easily.

7. You can share a beer with your friends.

8. A beer is always wet.

9. Beer doesn't demand equality.

10. A beer doesn't care when you come home.

The Youngest Child

She lay nude between the sheets
And I beside her lay;
And she was soft and round and chubby,
Under my hand uprose her bubby.

My hand beneath her waist did stroke,
Her tip-tops itched and tingled,
I clambered up, began to poke,
And our juices intermingled.

'Pull out!' Pull out!' the fair one cried,
'Before I swell with trouble.'
I did. And on her snow white breast
My come did froth and bubble.

I gazed into her frightened eyes
And with the leery curse
'This is the youngest child,' I said,
'That you will ever nurse.'

She picked it up with one fair hand,
And with a shocked 'Oh La!'
She threw the load into my face,
Saying, 'Child, go kiss your Pa!'

THE DISAGREEMENT.

The Tree of Life

Come prick up your ears, and attend Sirs, awhile;
I'll sing ye a song that'll cause ye to smile;
'Tis a faithful description of the tree of life,
So pleasing to ev'ry maid, widow and wife.

This tree it a succulent plant I declare,
Consisting of only one straight stem, I swear,
Its top sometimes looks like a cherry in May,
At other times more like a filbert they say.

This tree universal all countries produce,
But till eighteen years growth 'tis not much fit for
    use;
Then nine or ten inches – it seldom grows higher,
And that's sure as much as the heart can desire.

Its juice taken inward's a cure for the spleen,
And removes in an instant the sickness called
    Green;
Tho' sometimes it causes large tumors below,
They disperse of themselves in nine months or so.

It cures all dissensions 'twixt husband and wife,
And makes her look pleasant through each stage
    of life,
By right application it never can fail,
But then it is always put in through the tail.

Ye Ladies that long for the sight of this tree,
Take this invitation – come hither to me,
I have it just now at the height of perfection,
Adjusted for handling and fit for injection!

The Puritanical Mathyas

There was a puritanical lad
And he was called Mathyas,
Who wished to go to Amsterdam
To speak with Annayas.
He had not gone past half a mile,
But he met a holy sister,
He laid his bible under her c**t,
And merrily he kissed her.

'Alas! what would the wicked say?'
Said she, 'if they had seen it!
My buttocks need some bolstering,
So put the Gospels in it!
'But peace sweetheart, for ere we part
– I speak from pure devotion
– By aye or nay I'll not away.
Until you taste my motions.'

They made full stride with many a heave,
Until they both were tired,
'Alas', said she, 'you f**k with glee,
And my petticoats are all mired.
If we professors of the lamb
To the English congregation,
Either at Leyden or Amsterdam,
It would disgrace the nation.'

'But since it is, that part we must
Though I am much unwilling,
Good brother have another thrust,
And take from me this shilling,
To pay your way for many a day
And feed you prick with filling.'
Then down she laid, the holy maid.
And drained him at a sitting.

O'Reilly's Daughter

Sitting in O'Reilly's bar,
Drinking beer and passing water,
Suddenly a thought came to my mind,
'How about shagging O'Reilly's daughter?'

CHORUS

Yipee-ai-ay, yipee-ai-oh,
Yipee-ai-ay to the one-eyed Reilly,
Rub it up, stuff it up, balls and all
Hey jig-a-jig, shag on.

Well, up the stairs and into bed,
Soon I had my right leg over.
Not a word the maiden said,
Laughed like hell when it all was over.

CHORUS

I shagged her standing,
I shagged her lying,
If I'd had wings I'd have shagged her flying.

CHORUS

I heard a footstep on the stairs,
Who should it be but the one-eyed Reilly,
Ruddy great pistols in his hand,
Looking for the man who'd shagged his daughter.

CHORUS

I grabbed O'Reilly by the hair,
Stuffed his head in a bucket of water,
Stuffed his pistols up his arse,
A damn sight quicker than I shagged his
daughter.

CHORUS

Now O'Reilly's dead and gone,
Did we bury him? Not likely,
Nailed his arse to the shit house door,
And now we bugger him twice nightly.

CHORUS

There was a young plumber of Lea,
Who was plumbing a girl by the sea.
She said 'Stop your plumbing,
there's somebody coming',
Said the plumber, still plumbing, 'It's me!'

Sunny Side of Jermyn Street

It nearly broke her Mother's heart,
When Mary Jane became a tart,
But blood is blood and race is race,
And so to save the family face,
They bought her quite the nicest beat
On the sunny side of Jermyn Street.

It hardly took his Father's fancy,
When brother Claude became a nancy.
He thought their friends would all neglect 'em
If common chaps used young Claude's rectum.
So Claude he swore he'd hawk his steerage,
Exclusively among the peerage.

Her Ladyship abandoning caution,
Gave evening classes in abortion,
Her daughter, her first patient died
– She spent the next two years inside,
Poor father feeling rather limp
Regretfully became a pimp.

British Gonorrhoea

Some die of Diabetes and some of Diarrhoea,
Some die of drinking whisky and some of drinking
    beer,
But of all the world's diseases there's none that
    can compare
With the drip, drip, drip from the end of your prick
Of the British Gonorrhoea.

There was a young girl from Azores,
Whose c**t was covered in sores.
All the dogs in the street,
Would lick the green meat,
That hung in festoons from her drawers.

THE FOUL

The Sexual Desires of a Camel

To the Eton Boating Song.

The sexual desires of a camel
Are greater than anyone thinks.
At the height of the mating season
He copulates with the Sphinx.
But the Sphinx's vaginal organ
Is immersed in the sands of the Nile,
Which accounts for the hump on the camel
And the Sphinx's inscrutable smile.

1st CHORUS

Singing Bum Titty, Bum Titty, Titty Bum
Bum Titty Bum Titty ay,
Singing, Bum Titty, Bum Titty, Titty Bum,
Singing, Bum Titty Bum Titty ay.

Now the sexual life of an Ostrich,
Is hard to understand,
We know this remarkable creature,
Will bury itself in the sand
When another one comes up behind it,
And sees his great arse in the air,
Does he up with his chopper and grind it,
Or doesn't he f**king well care?

1st CHORUS

Oh, I went to ride on a puffer,
There was hardly room to stand,
A little boy offered his seat,
So I grabbed it with both hands.

'Cos we're all queers together,
That's why we go round in pairs.
Yes we're all queers together,
Excuse us while we go upstairs.

Oh my name is Cecil,
I live in Leicester Square,
I walk down Piccadilly,
With a rosebud in my hair,

2nd CHORUS

Oh my name is Basil,
My friend's name is Bond,
We're always together,
That's why we're called Basildon Bond.

2nd CHORUS

It was Christmas day in the Harem
The eunuchs all sat on the stairs,
Watching the dusky maidens
Combing their golden hair.
Then suddenly the voice of the Sultan
Came booming through the halls
Singing 'What do you want for Christmas?'
The eunuchs all answered, 'Balls!'

2nd CHORUS

My Grandfather's Cock

My Grandfather's cock was too large for his wife
So he used it on the woman next door.
It was taller by half than the old man himself
And it weighed half a hundredweight more.
He had the horn on the morn of the day that he
    was born
It was always his pleasure and his pride.
But it dropped, flopped never to rise again
When the old man died.

Ninety years without fumbling,
Flip flop, flip flop,
His life seconds numbering,
Flip flop, flip flop,
But it dropped, flopped, never to rise again,
When the old man died.

Nine Old Ladies

Oh dear what can the matter be,
Nine old ladies locked in the lavatory,
They were there from Sunday to Saturday,
Nobody knew they were there.

The first was the Bishop of Chichester's daughter.
She only went there to get rid of some water,
But she got involved with a Billingsgate Porter
And nobody knew she was there.

CHORUS

The second one was called Elizabeth Fender,
She went in there to adjust her suspender
She got it all mixed with the feminine gender
And nobody knew she was there

CHORUS

The third one was called Elizabeth Humphrey
She went in there and felt ever so comfy,
She tried to get up but could not get her bum free
And nobody knew she was there

CHORUS

The fourth one was called Elizabeth Prior
She wasn't a goer but she was a trier
The level of water rose higher and higher
And nobody knew she was there

CHORUS

The fifth one was called Elizabeth Petter
She only went there to extract a French Letter
But when she got there she found Rendell's were
    better
And nobody knew she was there

CHORUS

The sixth one was called Elizabeth Draper
She was afraid the Bishop would rape her
So she stuffed up her arse with lavatory paper
And nobody knew she was there

CHORUS

The seventh one was called Elizabeth Carter
She was the ladies World Champion Farter,
She went there to render the Moonlight Sonata
And nobody knew she was there

CHORUS

The eighth one was called Elizabeth Howell
She only went there to inspect her san-towel
She'd had it four weeks, it was perfectly foul
And nobody knew she was there

CHORUS

The last was the famous Countess Dubarry
She only went in to adjust her pessary
But all that she found was the Colonel's Glengarry
Nobody knew he'd been there.

Wild West Show

CHORUS

We're going to the Wild West Show
To see the Elephants and the Kangaroo-oo-oo-oo,
Never mind the weather,
As long as we're together
We're going to the Wild West Show.
– And here we have:-

Winky Wanky bird – Its eyelids are stuck to its
foreskin, when it winks it wanks.

Elephant – largest mammal – shits a ton – stand
back lady too late – get a shovel and dig her out.

Wildcat – grows very wild when in the forest – no
arsehole – that's why.

Laughing Hyena – eats once a week, drinks once a
month, copulates once a year – I don't know
what he has to laugh about.

Camel – it is the ship of the desert – it turns to the
East and farts 4 times, turns to the west and farts
4 times – hence the Trade Winds.

Kee-Kee Bird – found at the North Pole resting on
an iceberg, saying 'Kee-Kee-Christ, it's cold!'

Rhinoceros – rhino- meaning money, ceros
meaning piles – piles of money.

Crocodile – it has the tightest skin – every time it
winks, it wanks – like the Winky Wanky bird –
don't throw sand in his eye, that ain't fair.

Kangaroo – every time it jumps, it farts. Every time it farts, it jumps, and this has puzzled the best scientific brains for years – is it farts that make it jump?

Oozlum Oozlum Bird – flies in ever decreasing circles eventually up its own arsehole, and in blue smoke it disappears, and from this advantageous postion it hurls shit and derision on its enemies.

Ibis-Ibis Bird – found in the Nile Delta – hence the pyramids and the Y.M.C.A.

Orang-Outan – with its blue aresehole swings from tree to tree etc

Farewell Bird – quiet flycatcher found skulking in the undergrowth, from whence it softly sings, 'Bye Bye! Bye Bye!' which being politely interpreted – means 'F**k – off'

'Oh-Ah' Bird – lays square eggs.

Giraffe – walk into an American Cocktail Bar – 'Highballs' on me.'

Porcupine – has 500 pricks – sorry madam! its prick is a teeny-weeny thing between its legs.

Arboretum – specimen trees – teak tree – used for cutting piles for piers, and by piles for Peers – I don't mean hairy haemorrhoids hanging from the hairy harseholes hof the Henglish Haristocracy!

'Inches'

Oh! I gave her inches one, drive it in, hammer it
    home,
Oh! I gave her inches one, drive it home,
Oh! I gave her inches one, she said, 'We've just
    begun
Put your belly close to mine, and waggle your bum,
    bum, bum.'

Inches two – she said, 'Try and follow through.'

Inches three – she said, 'Take your time from me.'

Inches four – she said, 'Work it up a little more.'

Inches five – she said, 'I'd wish you'd look alive.'

Inches six – she said, 'Try out all your tricks.'

Inches seven – she said, 'Keep it smooth and
    even.'

Inches eight – she said, 'Keep it strong and
    straight.'

Inches nine – she said, 'Now it's really fine.'

Inches ten – she said, 'I'm ready to start again.'

There was a Priest

There was a priest, the dirty beast,
Whose name was Alexander.
His mighty prick was inches thick
He called it Salamander.

One night he slept with a Gypsy Queen,
Whose face was black as charcoal
But in the dark he missed his mark,
And sparks came out of her arsehole.

A brat was born one rainy morn,
With a face as black as charcoal,
It had a prick ten inches thick
But it didn't have an arsehole.

The jolly Bishop of Birmingham,
He buggered three maids
    while confirming 'em.
As they knelt seeking God,
He excited his rod,
And pumped his episcopal sperm in 'em.

The Lobster

'Good morning Mr Fisherman,'
'Good morning Sir' said he,
'Have you a lobster, you could sell me?'

CHORUS

Singing roh-tiddle dee doh
Roh-tiddle dee doh (shit or bust)
Never let your bollocks
Dangle in the dust.

'Yes Sir, yes Sir, I have two,
The biggest of the bastards I will sell to you.'

CHORUS

So I took the lobster home,
And we didn't have a dish
So I put it in the pot
Where the missus used to piss.

CHORUS

Early next morning,
As you may know,
The missus arose,
To sit upon the po.

CHORUS

Now the lobster looked up,
With a smile on his kisser,
He grabbed the missus
In the middle of the pisser.

CHORUS

Now the missus gave a squeal,
The missus gave a grunt,
And she ran around the room,
With a lobster on her c**t.

CHORUS

Now I grabbed an axe,
And the missus grabbed a broom
And we chased the f**king lobster,
Round and round the room.

CHORUS

We beat him on the head,
We beat him on the side,
We beat the lobster on the balls
Until the bastard died.

CHORUS

The moral of this story,
Is plain to see,
Always have a shufty
Before you have a pee.

CHORUS

Your Spooning Days

Your spooning days are over,
Your pilot light is out,
What used to be your sex appeal,
Is now your water spout.

You used to be embarrassed
To make the thing behave,
For every blooming morning
It would stand up and watch you shave.

But now you are growing old
It sure gives you the blues,
To see the thing hang down your leg,
And watch you shine your shoes.

There was a young girl named McCall,
Whose c**t was exceedingly small.
But the size of her anus,
Was something quite heinous,
It could hold seven cocks and one ball.

The Harlot of Jerusalem

In the days of old there lived a maid,
She was the mistress of her trade,
A prostitute of high repute
The harlot of Jerusalem.

CHORUS

Hi ho Cathusalem,
Cathusalem, Cathusalem
Hi ho Cathusalem,
Harlot of Jerusalem.

And though she f**d for many a year
Of pregnancy she had no fear,
She washed her passage out with beer,
The best in all Jerusalem.

CHORUS:

Now in a hovel by the wall
A student lived with but one ball
Who'd been through all, or nearly all
The harlots of Jerusalem.

CHORUS

His phallic limb was lean and tall
His phallic art caused all to fall
And victims lined the Wailing Wall
That goes around Jerusalem.

CHORUS

One night returning from a spree,
His customary hard had he
And on the street he chanced to meet,
The harlot of Jerusalem.

CHORUS

Forth from the town he took the slut
For 'twas his whim always to rut,
By the Salvation Army hut
Outside of Old Jerusalem.

CHORUS

With artful eye and leering look,
He took out from its filthy nook,
His organ twisted like a crook
The pride of old Jerusalem.

CHORUS

He laid her down upon the grass,
Lifted her dress above her arse,
He grabbed his prick and made a pass
At the f**k hole of Jerusalem.

CHORUS

But she was low and underslung,
He missed her twat and hit her bung,
Planted the seeds of many a son,
In the arse-hole of Jerusalem.

CHORUS

It was a sight to make you sick,
To hear him grunt so fast and quick,
While rending with his crooked prick
The womb of fair Cathusalem.

CHORUS

Then up there came an Onanite,
With warty cock besmeared with shite
He'd sworn that he would gaol that night
The harlot of Jerusalem.

CHORUS

He loathed the act of copulation,
For his delight was masturbation
And with a spurt of cruel elation
He saw the whore Cathusalem.

CHORUS

So when he saw the grunting pair,
With roars of rage he rent the air,
And vowed that he would soon take care
Of the harlot of Jerusalem.

CHORUS

Upon the earth he found a stick
To which he fastened half a brick
And took a swipe at the mighty prick
Of the student of Jerusalem.

CHORUS

He seized the bastard by his crook,
Without a single furious look
And flung him over Kedron's brook
That bubbles past Jerusalem.

CHORUS

And feeling full of rage and fight
He pushed the bastard Onanite,
And rubbed his face in Cathy's shite
The foulest in Jerusalem.

CHORUS

Cathusalem she knew her part
She closed her c**t and blew a fart,
That sent him flying like a dart,
Right over old Jerusalem.

CHORUS

And buzzing like a bumble bee
He flew straight out to sea,
But caught his arse hole in a tree
That grows in old Jerusalem.

CHORUS

And to this day you can still see
His arse hole hanging from the tree
Let that to you a warning be
When passing through Jerusalem.

CHORUS

As for the student and his lass
Many a playful night did pass,
Until she joined the V.D. class
For harlots of Jerusalem.

CHORUS

She gave birth to illegits,
Little sluts with swinging tits
Who sold their slits for threepenny bits,
The harlots of Jerusalem.

CHORUS

There was a young man of high station,
Who was found by a pious relation,
Making love in a ditch,
To, I won't say a bitch,
But a woman of no reputation.

THE DECISION

How a Pussy was Made

Seven wise men made up their minds
To build them a pussy of their own design.
The first was a carpenter full of wit,
With a hammer and chisel he made the split.
The second a blacksmith black as coal,
With anvil and sledge he made the hole.
The third a tailor long and slim,
With a piece of red ribbon he lined it within.
The fourth a furrier big and stout,
With skin of a bear he lined it without.
The fifth a fisherman old and bent,
With a rotten herring he gave it a scent.
The sixth a doctor with no med-degree,
He petted it, felt it, and said it would pee.
The seventh a Rabbi, a mean little runt,
He f**ked it and blessed it and called it a c**t.

There was a full back named Ringer,
Who was screwing an opera singer.
Said he with a grin,
'Well, I've sure got it in!'
Said she, 'You mean that ain't your finger?'

Small Boys

Small boys are cheap today
Cheaper than yesterday
Small ones are half a crown
Standing up or lying down.
Big ones are four and six
'Cause they've got bigger dicks,
Small boys are cheap, cheaper today.

There was a young Scot from Delray,
Who buggered his father one day.
Saying, 'I like it rather,
To stuff it up father,
He's clean and there's nothing to pay.'

Lulu

Some girls work in factories
Some girls work in stores,
But some girls work in a knockin' shop
With forty other whores.

CHORUS

Oh bang away Lulu, bang away Lulu
Bang away good and strong,
Whata we to do for a good blow through,
When Lulu's dead and gone.

Lulu had a baby,
It was an awful shock
She couldn't call it Lulu 'cos
The bastard had a cock.

CHORUS

I took her to the pictures,
We sat down in the stalls,
And every time the lights went out
She grabbed me by the balls.

CHORUS

She and I went fishing
In a long poled punt
And every time I hooked a tiddler
She stuffed it up her c**t.

CHORUS

I wish I was a golden ring
Upon my Lulu's hand
And every time she scratched her c**t
I'd see the promised land.

CHORUS

I wish I was a chamber pot
Under Lulu's bed,
And every time she took a piss
I'd see her maidenhead.

CHORUS

The gay young Duke of Buckingham,
Stood on the bridge at Uppingham,
Watching the stunts,
Of the c**ts in the punts,
And the tricks of the pricks that were
    f***ing 'em.

THE PROTEST

Lydia Pinky

We'll drink, a drink, a drink,
To Lydia Pink, a Pink, a Pink,
Saviour of the human race,
For she invented a medicinal compound,
Most efficacious in every case.

My friend Denis had a very small penis
He could hardly raise a stand,
So they gave him the medicinal compound,
Now he comes in either hand.

CHORUS

Now Major Williams had very small knackers,
They were like a couple of peas,
So they gave him the medicinal compound
Now they hang below his knees.

CHORUS

Sister Glenis she had no Bristols,
She could hardly fill her blouse,
So they gave her the medicinal compound,
Now they milk her with the cows.

CHORUS

Brother Eric lacked hair on his bollocks
And his pecker wouldn't peck,
So they gave him medicinal compound,
Now he can wrap it round his neck.

CHORUS

Roll Me Over

Oh this is number one, and the fun has just begun,
Roll me over, lay me down and do it again.

CHORUS

Roll me over in the clover,
Roll me over, lay me down and do it again.

Oh this is number two, and my hand is on her
   shoe....
Oh this is number three, and my hand is on her
   knee....
Oh this is number four, and we're rolling on the
   floor....
Oh this is number five, and the bee is in the hive....
Oh this is number six, and she said she liked my
   tricks....
Oh this is number seven, and we're in seventh
   heaven....
Oh this is number eight, and the nurse is in the
   gate....
Oh this is number nine, and the twins are doing
   fine....
Oh this is number ten, and we're at it once again....
Oh this is number twenty, and she said that that
   was plenty....
Oh this is number thirty, and she said that that was
   dirty....
Oh this is number forty, and she said you are
   naughty....

Alluette

Alluetta, jaunte alluetta
Alluetta, jaunte plumerie

How I love your stringy hair

How I love your bloodshot eyes

How I love your snotty nose

How I love your craggy teeth

How I love your double chin

How I love your swinging tits

How I love your nebulous navel

How I love your hairy arse

How I love your knocking knees

How I love your sweaty feet

How I love your itchy crutch
Oh so very much.

Cuckoo Song

(Tune: Away in a manger.)

A strange bird is the cuckoo
As it sits on the grass,
With its wings neatly folded
And its beak up its arse.

In this strange position
It can only say "Twit,"
For its hard to say "Cuckoo"
With a beak full of shit.

The owl is a funny bird
With its eyes big and round,
And an uglier bastard
Can scarcely be found.

It flies through the night sky
Going "Tu whit, tu woo,"
Which in owl type language
Means, "Bollocks to you."

A mathematician named Hall,
Had a hexahedronical ball,
And the cube of it's weight,
Times his pecker times eight,
Was four-fifths of five eighths of f**k all.

WHAT . . . . . . ME?

Breakfast Song

(Introduction to Balls to Mr Banglestein)

The bell was sounded for breakfast
By the butler so portly and stout,
Father came down with his prick in his hand
And ma with her tits hanging out,
"Behave yourself nicely my children
Good manners have long been our boast."
"Good manners be buggered," said Thomas,
As he tossed off all over the toast.
Stan stuffed a sausage up Susan
And laughed long and hard at the joke,
Mother asked farther to fart in her hand
So the baby could play with the smoke.
The family were seated at breakfast
When Sammy threw porridge at the walls,
Father got up to say grace
And all the family said, "Balls!"

Balls to Mr. Banglestein

Balls to Mr. Banglestein, Banglestein, Banglestein,
Balls to Mr. Banglestein dirty old sod
He sits on the steeple,
And shits on the people
So balls to Mr. Banglestein, dirty old sod.

PAUSE . . .

CHANTED: A prayer for the constipated.

CHORUS: SHIT!

CHANTED: A prayer for the frustrated.

CHORUS: F**K!

CHANTED: A prayer for the castrated.

CHORUS: BALLS! to Mr. Banglestein etc. etc.

The Threshing Machine

'Twas way down in Devon that I did hear tell,
I first set my eyes on our little Nell,
She was so pretty and only sixteen,
When I ups and I shows 'er my Threshing Machine.

CHORUS

I 'ad 'er, I 'ad 'er, I' ad 'er I ay,
I 'ad 'er, I 'ad 'er, I' ad 'er I ay,
I' ad 'er by night and I' ad 'er by day,
And I ups and I shows 'er the West Country way.

The barn door was open and I steps inside,
Some hay in the corner I espied,
She worked the throttle and I worked the steam,
When I ups and I shows 'er my Threshing Machine.

CHORUS

Oh father, oh father, I've come to confess,
I've left a young maid in a hell of a mess,
Her blouse is all tattered, her tits are all bare,
And there's something inside her that shouldn't be
    there.

CHORUS

Oh son, oh son, you should have known better,
To woo a fair maid without a french letter,
Oh father, oh father, you do me unjust,
I used one of yours and the f**king thing bust.

CHORUS

Six months later all is not well,
The poor little maid is beginning to swell,
And under her apron can clearly be seen,
The terrible works of my Threshing Machine.

CHORUS

Nine months later all has gone well,
A new little babe for our little Nell,
And under his nappy can clearly be seen,
A brand new two cylinder Threshing Machine.

CHORUS

There was a young lady from Exeter,
So pretty, that men craned their
    necks at her.
One silly young sod,
Got thrown into quad,
For waving his organ of sex at her.

THE PENALTY.

The Happy Family

Air: Deutschland Uber Alles

Life presents a doleful picture,
All around is murk and gloom;
Father has an anal stricture,
Mother has a fallen womb.
In a corner sits Jemina,
Never laughs and rarely smiles;
What a dismal occupation,
Cracking ice for Father's piles.

Cousin James has been deported,
For a homosexual crime:
While the housemaid has aborted,
For the Twenty-second time.
Bill the baby's no exception,
For he's always having fits;
Every time he laughs he vomits,
Every time he farts – he shits.

Cousin Jo has won the Hackney
Masturbation marathon,
But has died of self-expression
Since he buggered Uncle Tom.
Bert the postman called this morning,
Stuck his penis through the door,
We could not, despite endearment,
Get it out till half past four.

In a small brown paper parcel,
Wrapped in a mysterious way,
Is an imitation arsehole
Granpaw uses twice a day.
From the boghouse hear him yelling,
No one helps the ancient lout,
For the plug is in his arsehole,
And he cannot get it out.

The Maid of the Mountain Glen

There was a maid of the mountain Glen,
Seduced herself with a fountain pen.
The pen it broke and the ink ran wild,
And she gave birth to a blue-black child.

CHORUS

They called the bastard Stephen,
They called the bastard Stephen,
They called the bastard Stephen,
For that was the name of the ink.

Stephen was a bonny child,
Pride and joy of his mother mild,
And all that worried her was this –
His steady stream of blue-black piss.

CHORUS

There was a young lady called Howells,
Who fed all day on pigs' bowels.
When she ran out of this
She drank prostitute piss
And the scrapings from sanitary towels.

The Red Flag

The working class
Can kiss my arse
I've got the foreman's job at last.
I'm out of work,
And on the dole
You can stuff the red flag
Up your hole.

'Twas on Gibraltar's rock, so fair,
I saw a maiden lying there
And as she lay in sweet repose,
A puff of wind blew up her clothes.
A sailor who was passing by
Tipped his hat and winked his eye.
And then he saw to his despair
She had the red flag flying there.

A young man from Aberystwith,
Fell out with a girl he played whist with,
When she trumped his trick
He took out his prick
And stuffed up the hole that she
    pissed with.

All the Nice Girls
Love a Candle

All the nice girls love a candle,
All the nice girls love a wick.
For there's something about a candle
Which reminds them of a prick.
Nice and greasy, slips in easy,
It's a girly's pride and joy.
It's been up our Lady Jane
And it's going up again,
Ship ahoy, ship ahoy.

There was a young lady from Bude,
She went to the flicks in the nude
A chappie up front said
"I can smell c**t,
Just like that, right out loud, f**king rude."

The Alphabet

A is for Arsehole all covered in shit, Hey ho, said
  Roley,
and B is the Bugger who revels in it,

CHORUS

With a Roley Poley up 'em and stuff 'em
Hey Ho said Anthony Roley.

C is for C**t all dripping with piss, Hey Ho said
  Roley,
and D is for Drunkard who gives it a kiss.

CHORUS

E is for Eunuch with only one ball, Hey Ho said
  Roley,
and F is for F****r with no balls at all,

CHORUS

G is for Gonorrhoea, Goitre & Gout, Hey Ho said
  Roley,
and H is for Harlots that spread it about,

CHORUS

I is injection for clap, pox and itch, Hey Ho said
  Roley,
and J is the jerk of a dog on a bitch,

CHORUS

K is the King who thought f*****g a bore, Hey Ho
  said Roley,
and L for Lesbian who came back for more,

CHORUS

M is for Maidenhead all tattered and torn, Hey Ho said Roley,
and N is for Noble who died with a horn,

CHORUS

O is for Orifice open and wide, Hey Ho said Roley,
and P is for Penis that slips up inside,

CHORUS

Q is Quaker who shat in his hat, Hey ho said Roley,
and R is the Rector who rogered the cat,

CHORUS

S is for Shit pot all filled to the brim, Hey Ho said Roley,
and T is the Turds that are floating within,

CHORUS

U is for Usher who taught us at school, Hey Ho said Roley,
and V is for Virgins that play with his tool,

CHORUS

W is a Whore who thinks f**king's a farce, Hey Ho said Roley,
and X, Y & Z you can stuff up your arse,

CHORUS

Why was he Born so Beautiful?

Why was he born so beautiful?
Why was he born at all?
He's no f*****g use to anyone,
He's no f*****g use at all.

There was a Bohemian monk,
Who slept all night in his bunk.
He dreamt of a venus
Who tickled his penis,
And woke up all covered in spunk.

'Help'

As I was walking through a wood
I shat myself – I knew I would.
I cried for help – but no help came.
And so I shat myself again.

There was a young man from Kent
Whose tool was exceedingly bent,
So to save himself trouble
He put it in double,
And instead of coming he went.

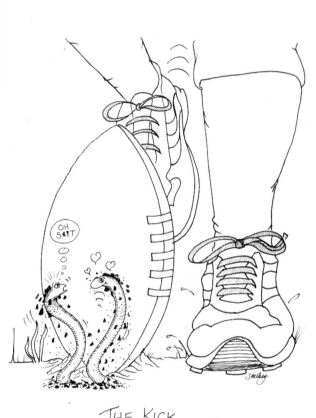

THE KICK

No Balls at All

Come on you old Drunkards give ear to my tale,
This short little story will make you turn pale,
It's about a young lady – so pretty and small
Who married a man who had no balls at all.

CHORUS

Balls, Balls
No balls at all,
She married a man
Who had no balls at all.

How well she remembered the night they were
    wed,
She rolled back the sheets and crept into bed.
She felt for his penis, how strange, it was small,
She felt for his balls, he had no balls at all.

CHORUS

Mummy, Oh Mummy, Oh pity my luck,
I've married a man who's unable to f**k.
His tool bag is empty, his screwdriver's small,
The impotent wretch has no nuts at all.

CHORUS

Oh daughter, my daughter, now don't be sad
I had the same trouble with your dear Dad,
There's many a man who'll come to the call
Of the wife of a man who's got no balls at all.

CHORUS

The pretty young girl took her mother's advice
And found the whole thing exceedingly nice.
An eleven-pound baby was born in the fall,
But the poor little bastard had no balls at all.

CHORUS

There was a young man from Cosham,
Who took out his bollocks to wash 'em.
His wife called out "Jack,
If you don't put them back,
I'll tread on the things and I'll squash 'em."

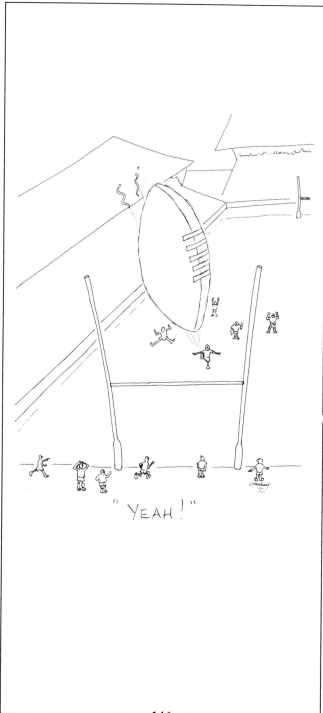

The Woodpecker Song

I put my finger in the woodpecker's hole,
And the woodpecker said, "God bless my soul,
Take it out, take it out, take it out, remove it."

I removed my finger from the woodpecker's hole,
And the woodpecker said, "God bless my soul,
Put it back, put it back, put it back, replace it."

I replaced my finger in the woodpecker's hole,
And the woodpecker said, "God bless my soul,
Turn it round, turn it round, turn it round, revolve it."

I revolved my finger in the woodpecker's hole,
And the woodpecker said, "God bless my soul,
Pull it out, pull it out, pull it out, retract it."

I retracted my finger from the woodpecker's hole,
And the woodpecker said, "God bless my soul,
Take a whiff, take a whiff, take a whiff,
    REVOLTING."

There was a policeman from Clapham Junction
Whose tool just wouldn't function.
So he fooled his wife
For the rest of his life,
With some snot on the end of his truncheon.

Show me the Way to Go Home

Show me the way to go home,
I'm tired and I wanna go to bed,
I had a little drink about an hour ago,
And it's gone right to my head.
No matter where I roam, over land or sea or foam,
You will always hear me singing this song,
Show me the way to go home.

She wears her silk pyjamas in the summer when
it's hot.
She wears her woollen nighty in the winter when
it's not.
But sometimes in the springtime and sometimes in
the fall,
She slips between the sheets with nothing on at
all.

She's a most immoral lady,
She's a most immoral lady,
She's a most immoral lady,
And she lay between the sheets with nothing on at
all.

REPEAT 1ST VERSE

Oh Sir Jasper do not touch me,
Oh Sir Jasper do not touch me,
Oh Sir Jasper do not touch me,
And she lay between the sheets with nothing on at
all.

REPEAT 1ST VERSE

Glory, Glory Hallelujah,
See the devil coming to yuh,
He's gonna put his prick right through yuh
For jumping into bed with nothing on at all.

THE WORLD CUP 1991
RUGBY SONGS
&
DITTIES

If you would like to acquire additional copies of this
book, please complete this coupon and send to:

World Cup Projects,
FREEPOST
PLYMOUTH
PL1 1BR

Please make cheques/postal orders payable to:
World Cup Projects.

I would like to receive .... copies of The
1991 Rugby World Cup Song & Ditty Book at a unit
price of £4.60 inc p&p

I enclose a cheque for the sum of £ ....

Name ....
Address ....
....
Tel. No (daytime) ....

✂

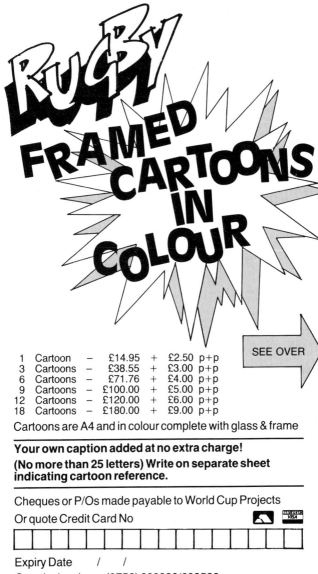

RUGBY FRAMED CARTOONS IN COLOUR

SEE OVER →

1	Cartoon	–	£14.95	+	£2.50 p+p
3	Cartoons	–	£38.55	+	£3.00 p+p
6	Cartoons	–	£71.76	+	£4.00 p+p
9	Cartoons	–	£100.00	+	£5.00 p+p
12	Cartoons	–	£120.00	+	£6.00 p+p
18	Cartoons	–	£180.00	+	£9.00 p+p

Cartoons are A4 and in colour complete with glass & frame

Your own caption added at no extra charge!
(No more than 25 letters) Write on separate sheet indicating cartoon reference.

Cheques or P/Os made payable to World Cup Projects

Or quote Credit Card No

Expiry Date   /   /

Or order by phone (0752) 660030/603588

Signature   (I am over 18)

Mr/Mrs/Ms   (Block Capitals

Street

Town

Country   Post Code

World Cup Projects, FREEPOST, Plymouth PL1 1BR
Offer applies to UK only. Allow 21 days for delivery.
Overseas: Prices on application.

Quantity ☐ Quantity ☐

Quantity ☐ Quantity ☐

Quantity ☐ Quantity ☐

1 FIVE MINUTES TO GO

2 THE REF.

3 THE SKIPPER

4 THE DISAGREEMENT

5 THE DECISION

6 THE FOUL

Please indicate
cartoon required
and return with
order form

Quantity ☐

7

THE PROTEST

Quantity ☐

8

N° 8.

Quantity ☐

9

N° 9

Quantity ☐

10

FRONT ROW MAN

Quantity ☐

11

THE SUBSTITUTE

Quantity ☐

12

THE SCRUM

Please indicate cartoon required and return with order form

TEST YOUR WIT
WITH YOUR OWN VERSES. IF PUBLISHED WE WILL SEND YOU A FREE CARTOON OF YOUR CHOICE.

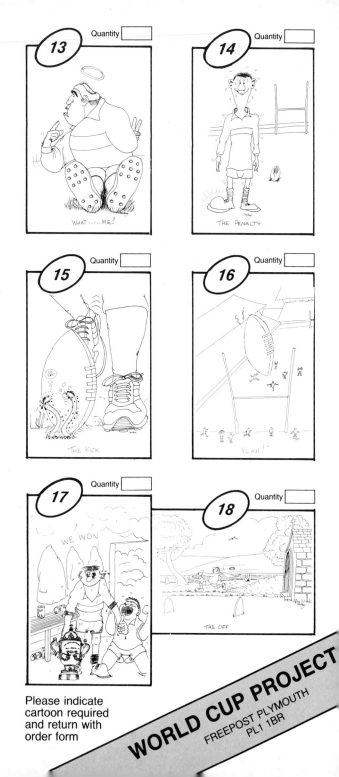

Please indicate
cartoon required
and return with
order form